Bud was a very special little guy. He had a way of making everyone he knew feel like he was their bird. His memory will be shared by many friends, which is all any of us can hope for when our time comes. He had one heck of a run. Here's to you, Bud.

Frank Urban
Onancock, VA

Distributed by
Bay Beyond Inc.
29368 Atlantic Dr.
Melfa, VA 23410 USA
1-800-221-2722
www.mybirdbud.com

Printed in the United States of America by
The MASA Corporation, Norfolk, Virginia.

Preface

Bud entered my life in 1992. I had not given much thought to adding a bird to our menagerie. We already had our black lab, Raven, a brown-colored cat appropriately named Brown, plus an assortment of Chesapeake Bay saltwater fish, shellfish and seahorses, gifts from a local waterman.

Chesapeake Bay seahorses

Pam and Raven

Our cat, Brown

Boo's Gift

In September 1992, an old college friend, nicknamed Boo, called from Chapel Hill. She was raising cockatiels and wanted to give me one. I'm the kind of person who has a hard time saying no. I visited Boo and her birds in North Carolina. A large cage in her kitchen held Mama Bird and two young 'tiels, hatched the previous year. Boo had taught Mama Bird to whistle the Andy Griffith Show theme song and the two youngsters had picked up the tune as well. Boo asked me to

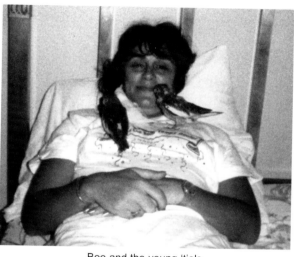

Boo and the young 'tiels

take both young cockatiels back to Virginia. She wanted me to pick out one to keep and find a home for the other.

My cousin Stephen, who lived nearby, gave me a hand-me-down cage. After a quick lesson in cockatiel care, including warnings about drafts, broken feathers and foods to avoid, I left Boo's and

headed to visit my folks, who also lived in North Carolina. I'll never forget that weekend in September. It was my father's 72nd birthday and the last time I ever saw him alive. For the next fourteen years, I linked this bird to my Dad. To me, that made him even more special.

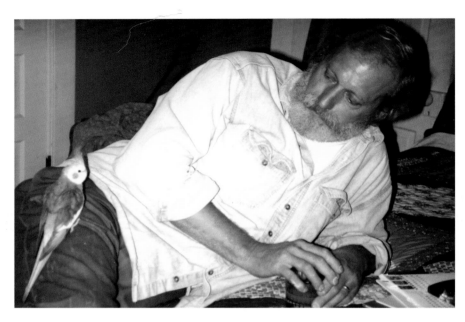

Returning to Onancock on Virginia's Eastern Shore, my husband Jim Green and I named one cockatiel Bud and the other Weiser. I chose Bud as the bird I would keep and gave Weiser to a friend who worked on Wallops Island at NASA.

Bud and Weiser entertain Mary

I placed Bud's cage on a cabinet in my office at my specialty foods business, Blue Crab Bay, and kept him fed and watered. I didn't touch him, and I didn't open the cage. He seemed to be as afraid of me as I was of him. I didn't have a clue how to tame him.

I remember thinking, based on my experience with a parakeet when I was a child: *It will be amazing if this bird survives a year.*

The Taming

About a month later, after Bud had survived on food and water in solitary confinement, I decided it was time to make friends. Through my research on cockatiels, I learned that they were very social and needed some free time outside their cage. My office had a large picture window with vertical blinds. On his first time out, I didn't want

any window crashes. I closed the blinds, placed his cage on the carpet and sat down on the floor. I spoke to him in a gentle voice and cautiously opened the cage door. Bud was panic stricken. He refused to get on my finger and attempted to bite me viciously. So much for hand fed 'tiels! I quickly wrapped my fingers around his body and removed him from the cage. He screamed and fussed but was helpless.

I continued to talk quietly, holding him tenderly against the leg of my jeans until he calmed down. Then I allowed him to return to his cage. Well, at least I got over my fear of touching him. We repeated that process a few times over the following weeks. Each time he seemed less afraid of my touch. Eventually he climbed willingly onto my two outstretched fingers.

Feeling more secure, I left his cage door open on the cabinet when I was in the office. My husband built a little cage-top playground for him, complete with a perch, swing, mirror and toys. Bud would climb out of his cage in the morning and stay on the playground all day long, only returning to the cage for a bite to eat, a few beak strokes against the cuttlebone or sips of water.

One day, I was sitting at my desk, typing. Bud flew over and landed on my arm. Then he looked up and bowed his head. I returned to typing, with him on my arm. Whenever I sensed him looking up, I would look down at him and he would immediately bow his head again. *What in the world is he doing?* Then it occurred to me, *he wants me to scratch his head!* So I reached over and

touched him. He turned his little head this way and that so I could scratch his orange cheeks and underneath his beak. Bud had tamed me.

That Bird in the Mirror

I never knew that a bird could enjoy his reflection so much. Once I realized how much Bud loved looking at "that bird in the mirror," I bought various sized mirrors to have on hand, no matter where he was. There was a little round one hanging inside his cage, and another on top of the playground.

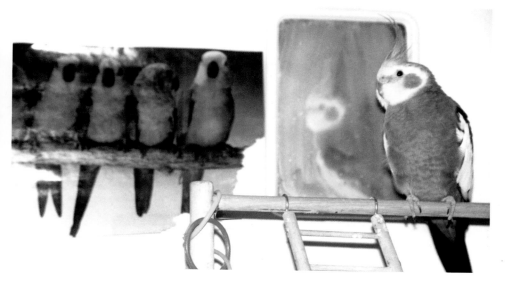

I found a vintage brass cage with a floor stand at an antique shop in Delaware and took that home to serve as the weekend cottage. I also brought home a wicker picnic basket from a trip to New York City. Inside the basket, I placed a rear view mirror which had broken off my van in a car wash. For many years, Bud traveled back and forth from work to home in this basket.

Nearly every Friday afternoon, I placed the picnic basket on top of my desk. Bud would fly over and climb inside to greet that "bird in the mirror" who he had missed terribly. All the way home, he would whistle the Andy Griffith Show theme song, thrilled to be in the car with his friend. Sometimes I would stop by the supermarket, and if it was too cold or too hot to leave him in the car, I would place the picnic basket in my grocery cart and off we would go. More than once, heads turned when they heard that familiar whistled tune. They had no idea where it was coming from.

Arriving home, I lift the basket's lid for Bud to climb out. He'd fly over to his cottage, enter the cage and greet another old friend in the mirror that hung inside. It seemed that every mirror reflected a different bird. He had so many friends!

Whenever I walked around with him on my shoulder, if we passed a mirror, I had to stop so he could see the other bird. He enjoyed his kitchen sink baths a lot more if a friend was there. And once I learned how much he enjoyed getting in the shower with me, I had to locate yet another mirror.

Frightful Things

If you've ever owned a cockatiel, you probably know about night frights. According to the books, this is something that happens in the middle of the night when it's dark and some little noise or imagined terror spooks the bird. They thrash their wings around madly, scared witless. At work, I stopped covering Bud's cage at night so he could see what was happening.

Anita, one of our production staff, stayed late one evening to do some vacuuming. Now, I do not have any idea how someone can vacuum an office without turning on the lights. But Anita could, and evidently did. That particular evening, something in my dark office flew through her hair and came back at her again. She flailed her arms around like someone attacked by bats. Then she turned on the lights. It was Bud. Someone forgot to close his cage door.

At home, his cage was just outside our bedroom. I wanted Bud to sleep soundly and not wake me singing his tunes at the break of dawn, so I covered his cage every evening with a large, dark blue piece of fabric.

Bud hated flies. If one flew into my office and came near his cage, he would cock his head to the side, cautiously eyeing the fly. Then he would hiss up a storm and dart around on the cage top, attempting to dodge the little winged beast. Another thing that spooked Bud was crows. He hated the sound of crows. Sometimes he would see or hear the big black cackling monsters fly by my office window, and he would panic, circling the room in flight.

On the weekends, I would place his cage on a table on our screened porch and open his door. He loved to sit on top of the cage, watching hummingbirds and butterflies pass by. He became very agitated, however, when preying mantises flew up on the screen.

For about half of his life, I kept his wings clipped. He could still fly, although low and slow. As years passed, I didn't clip his wings as often. He could fly fast and would do so if frightened or just showing off. Occasionally he would fly into the window or glass door, always leaving a dusty print of wings on the glass. Fortunately he never hurt himself. I always thought that the imprint looked like angel wings.

I had no idea that a bird raised in captivity didn't like anything that resembled a snake. On one occasion, I came into my office to find Bud sitting on his playground perch with no top feathers on his head. On the floor was a pile of long slender yellow feathers. Curled up on top of my conference table was a bright orange extension cord. Linda, our operations manager, had brought it into my office so I could take it to a trade show. I asked her what had happened. She said that Bud flew around the room and bumped his head feathers against the blades of the ceiling fan, which fortunately wasn't on. (I never ran it when he was out of his cage).

On my 50th birthday, the staff filled my office full of black helium balloons. Needless to say, they removed Bud and his cage before doing so. Can you imagine the terror that would have caused?

I'll never forget the day Allen, a salesman from our local radio station, was seated in a chair near my desk, describing an upcoming promotion. From his cage-top playground, Bud stared curiously at Allen then flew in circles around the room, buzzing Allen's head. After awhile he landed on Allen's shoulder, cocked his head and glared at Allen's chest. We were both confused. *What was going on in this bird's mind?*

Then I laughed, "Allen, it's your necktie, Bud thinks it's a snake!" Allen quickly grabbed his necktie and waved it around, exclaiming, "This old thing?" At which point Bud totally flipped out and flew into a window, crashing to the floor, uninjured. From that day forward Allen was always known as the "Snake Man".

Mashed Potatoes & Steamed Blues

We could never eat alone when Bud was around. He insisted on being with us, exploring and tasting whatever was on our plates. If you put him in another room, he fussed and fussed because he could smell the food. I guess you would call him a spoiled bird. We knew to keep him away from things like avocados and chocolate, but just about everything else was fair game.

Bud was very picky about what commercial bird food he would eat. I typically bought a brand name seed mixture for cockatiels, and he would selectively pick out the sunflower seeds and other small favorite seeds to eat. At work and at home, I would toss his leftovers out to the wild birds. The doves loved it.

Bud's three favorite foods were mashed potatoes, raw broccoli and steamed Blue Crabs. At work, he would fly over to my desk to taste whatever I had on my plate, even chicken or beef. Sometimes I would stop by a fast food restaurant and buy a small container of mashed potatoes. As soon as I walked into the office, he would start screeching, he could smell them.

Michael & Bud pick crabs

Three young sportsmen camped in our yard after a day of wild turkey hunting. They grilled turkey breast and made fresh mashed potatoes. Bud was home that weekend and flew over to the table where we were dining. He hopped around from shoulder to shoulder, looking for a handout. One of the young men put a little dab of mashed potatoes on the shoulder of his shirt and Bud ate it quickly. This routine continued again and again, until finally Bud turned around, took a poop on the guy's shoulder, then turned back around, thinking it was another dab of potatoes. He picked it up, quickly realized what it was and flung it against the guy's cheek! We shared a hearty laugh.

Bud loved it when we steamed Blue Crabs that we caught off our dock. He would walk all over the crabs, picking at bits of shell.

He also enjoyed anything salty like peanuts, chips and crackers. He loved our company's spicy Crab House® peanuts and our snack mix Barnacles®. His photo occasionally appeared in our mail order catalog since he was such a big fan.

One year Bud made the big time. His photo appeared in a special article about the positive power of office pets in a 1993 issue of the national magazine *Cooking Light*. He even signed a photo release and received a check for $25. He was also featured in our local electric co-op magazine and an *Eastern Shore News* article about pets.

FOWLshots

1 POLLY WANNA CRAB LEG – Bud is VP of Noise & Commotion at Blue Crab Bay Co. on the Eastern Shore. From Bud's buddy, N & C President Pam Barefoot of Melfa.

Courtesy ANEC Cooperative Living Magazine

Games Bud Played

It was nearly impossible to hold a serious meeting in my office when Bud was playing his games. One performance was the Soaring Eagle. He would lean over from his high perch, stretch out his wings and pretend to soar. If music was playing, he would dance back and forth on the perch, moving to the beat of the music.

by buttons

My favorite bird game was Dodge Ball. I would be preoccupied with a business call or paperwork and Bud would want attention. To get it, he would start screeching. He would screech and screech from the top of his playground perch. I would reach into my waste can, pull out a piece of paper and crumple it into a ball, then pretend that I was going to throw it at him. His head feathers would perk up and he would run and hide behind all of the toys that were hanging above his perch. He would cautiously peek out his head from one side, then the other hoping I would actually toss it.

Another game he played was Drop the Paper. I would put several pieces of old business letterhead on top of his playground. He would pick up each piece, walk over to the side and drop it, watching it slowly drift to the floor. This game grew tiresome for me and I was glad when he forgot about it. Too much work!

A really fun game happened when I placed an empty soft drink case on top of his playground, open at one end. Bud would go inside and peek out of any holes that were in the sides of the box. Sometimes he could be very protective of the box and would hiss angrily if you came near.

In the winter, I often wore a turtleneck under a sweater. Bud would climb up under my sweater and go from the bottom of it up to my neck, where he would proudly emerge from his journey. Folks were usually astonished to see a lump moving up under my clothing, especially when I told them it was Bud playing the

Sweater Game. The key to playing this game was to make sure he stayed between the turtleneck and the sweater as his claws were very sharp.

Another game Bud enjoyed was Wring My Neck. Visitors would be in my office, and he would start making loud noises, obviously trying to get attention. I would sternly say, "Bud, if you don't stop that, I'm going to wring your neck." Of course, he didn't stop, so I would get up, go over to his cage, put my fingers gently around his neck and pretend to wring it. My guests looked on in horror, actually believing I was strangling my bird! Bud loved it, he got the attention he was craving.

Betsy, a former Blue Crabber

The Love Bird

In the springtime when Bud was young, he always fell in love. One year it was with a wooden crab mallet, the next year a nautical dish towel. If you showed him these objects, he would coo over them and act like a love struck teen. Our label supplier, Wayne, sent Bud a couple of poems he wrote about these special times:

Spring's in the air,
We're such a pair,
So watch the skies,
for a mallet that flies.

This year his heart and tail do wag,
His love this time, a real dish rag.
If what he's doing is sowing seeds of youth,
It's not Letterman you need but Dr. Ruth!

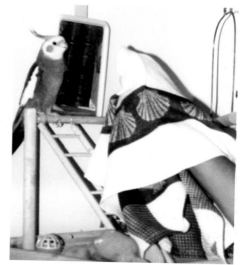

Bud was obsessed with men. And he always remembered the ones he liked. Our company artist, Michael, would pass through twice a year en route to or from his sailboat in the Caribbean and his home in Canada. Bud was always thrilled to see him.

Michael and Bud

And then there was Biggy, a gentle older man with a vision problem. He worked for the local dry cleaners, picking up clothing from businesses. Someone else had to drive him around, since he was nearly blind. Biggy had a booming voice. When he entered our shop, even though it was five offices away from mine, Bud would chirp loudly. Biggy would find his way down the long hallway to my office, then hold out his large hand. He was never quite sure where Bud was located, but Bud would move over to the outstretched hand and hold down his head so Biggy could scratch it.

Bud loved getting his head scratched. He would check out each person who entered my office, decide if he liked them enough, then jump on their shoulder and hold his head down. As he was quite sociable, he would allow just about anyone to touch him. He was, however, wary of young children with uncontrollable arms.

Dawn, our financial manager, often brought her two young children to our kid-friendly workplace. Her son, DJ, first met Bud in 1992 when Bud was a year old and DJ was three. DJ would wander down the hallway to my office, fascinated with Bud. At first Bud was frightened of DJ's waving arms, but DJ eventually learned to move quietly. And Bud learned to trust him. He would hop on DJ's shoulder and the two of them would go for a walk around the offices. They grew up together: DJ was a high school senior when we lost Bud.

DJ's sister, Stephanie

Close Calls

Initially I found myself over-protective. I was afraid to let Bud out of the cage. My cousin Michael trusted his cockatiel enough to take her outside on his shoulder. However, she flew up into a tree and he never saw her again. I often saw classified ads in newspapers that read Lost Cockatiel. I was determined that wouldn't

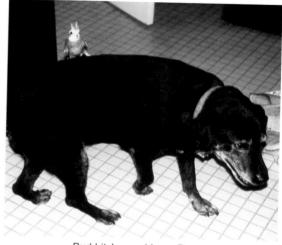
Bud hitches a ride on Raven

happen to Bud. I also knew that in order for him to be truly happy, he needed some freedom, and I needed to trust him.

Looking back, it's amazing Bud lived so long. There were many close calls, despite my concern for his safety. Shortly after I first brought him home, he disappeared when I left the cage door open. We found him, underneath our brass bed along with Brown, our cat. They were just sitting there, staring at each other. Luckily for Bud, Brown was a rescue,

Isaeva, Mario and Bud

a poor stray who had no teeth and was frightened of everything. Bud had no fear of our elderly black Lab, Raven, and he frequently would fly over to Raven's back and take a ride.

Years later, we moved to our new home on a secluded waterfront peninsula with Isaeva, our new black Lab, and Mario, a large yellow cat. We adopted Mario from the SPCA just after 9/11 and named him in honor of New York's governor. He was a born hunter, frequently bringing home small wildlife. I was always careful to make sure that Mario and Bud were never in the same room together when Bud was loose.

There came a day when Mario was asleep on the sofa. I took Bud's cage to the master bath and placed it on the shower floor. I opened the cage door and closed the doors to the bathroom, the hallway and the bedroom. Three doors between Mario and Bud, the free bird. I was preoccupied with phone calls and computer work when I suddenly noticed that Mario was no longer on the sofa. My heart nearly stopped as I saw the bedroom door ajar. *Did I leave it that way?* And then the hallway door, also open, and the bathroom sliding door, open enough. The horror of what could await me began sinking in. My heartbeat pounded in my ears. How could I get so distracted and forget about my Bud???

I opened the door a bit further and looked into the shower. There sat Mario, beside Bud's cage. There sat Bud, on top of his cage, curiously eyeing Mario. I immediately swooped in, grabbed Mario and took him outside, my adrenaline racing.

A few years before, in my office at Blue Crab Bay where Bud always reigned free, someone unexpectedly walked in with a young yellow Lab. I was out of the office. The dog saw Bud and made a mad dash for the

bird cage. Bud was frantic and flew around the room in circles. Two employees saved the day, one by jumping with her entire body on top of the dog. The glass topped lobster-crate table with its potted plant turned over during the episode, soil flying everywhere. At least it wasn't feathers. I owed my staff, big time.

One sunny weekend, Bud was free on our screened porch, and our Lab, Isaeva, was asleep on the floor. Bud was always safe around Isaeva, as the only things she wanted to chase were balls or a Frisbee. Jim and I were invited to a dinner party nearby. Later that evening, while we were at the party, a large thunderstorm with lightning arrived unexpectedly. *Bud! I forgot to put Bud in the house! Wet drafts! Rain! Dog! Horrors! I'm going home now!* I quickly drove home and turned on the porch light. Isaeva was relieved to go back inside, as she was quite fearful of thunder. *But Bud, where is Bud?* I looked everywhere; I got on my hands and knees and looked under the wicker furniture. I could not find Bud. No feathers either. Then I heard a faint tweet. There he was, hidden in the foliage of the hanging plant.

A couple of times Bud escaped from the offices and made it into our large warehouse. The only way to get him back was to hold up a mirror. However, sometimes a mirror was useless, like when he landed behind a tall pallet of flat cardboard boxes or when he landed behind the kitchen stove, which was situated between a wall and the refrigerator. I remember our product manager, Frank, lifting the stove up so I could coax Bud out from behind it.

Where's Bud?

The Vice President of Noise & Commotion

At work, Bud was affectionately known as the Vice President of Noise and Commotion. He was even listed on our Organization Chart. Being a woman-owned and mostly woman-operated business, he was definitely one of the few guys around. He was more fond of men than women, adoring Frank, who cared for him when I traveled to food shows. Bud was also a great alarm system. When I arrived at work each morning, all of the employees knew I was there before I even parked the car. Bud let them know. He heard my particular vehicle coming and screeched with joy. *Was it joy or to let them know they better get to work 'cause the boss is here?* I often wondered.

When I opened my office door, he was already on his cage-top playground, thanks to my co-workers who let him out as soon as they

arrived to work. Our routine was a quick loving peck on the lips before I got to my desk, unless Bud was mad at me. On those days he would hiss. This happened sometimes when I returned from a weeklong trade show. He could get moody when he felt ignored; he would even bite my finger when he was angry. Never anyone else, just me. Don't bite the hand that feeds you? Bud didn't live by that rule.

Our intern, Casy

The entire staff helped take care of him, made sure he had food, water, and a clean cage when I traveled. If I was away over a long weekend, someone would take him to their home. When I called in from a trip, my first question was always *How's Bud?*

Kelley in the marketing office

To keep him company, Kelley would print out my photo and post it above his playground. Of course, he chewed it into pieces. If Bud wasn't on top of his cage when I arrived in the morning, I could usually find him cheerily perched on Frank or Kelley's shoulder, watching as they worked at their computers. He was a centerpiece at our staff meetings, always putting in his

two cents worth. At his last staff Christmas party, he was in a little travel cage with his own miniature Christmas tree. He wasn't just my bird, he was *our* bird.

I would be involved in new price lists, press releases, or product development. With my mind on work, I ignored Bud. He wouldn't let me get away with being too serious, however. He would fly over to my desk, pick up paper clips and start dropping them on the floor. He would try to give me a manicure, or dance on my electric typewriter (remember those?), leaving unreadable words. He would chew holes in my paperwork. Bud and I entered the computer age together. He loved pecking characters on the keyboard and freezing up the screen. If he still didn't have my complete attention, he would jump on my shoulder and start nibbling on my ear. Now who could resist the temptation to smile?

Eve from our sales department

David from the Chamber of Commerce

Lucille, our employee and also a client of the vocational center, worked for us nine years. Every day she took a break from labeling products to visit Bud in my office. He was always happy to see her as she greeted him in a deep and low voice, "Hello Frinny." A well-built gal, sometimes Lucille

brought her pet Beta fish to visit Bud. Usually Bud would fly across the room and skid onto Lucille's expansive chest much like a small jet landing on an aircraft carrier.

Our crab soup packer, Steve, came for a meeting. He had a head full of long, thick curls. While he was conversing with my operations manager and me, Bud flew over, landed on his head and hid quietly within the curls. No one said a word. The meeting continued. How could we not have laughed? And where was my camera? Bud loved to surprise our business visitors with an unexpected landing on their shoulders. And sometimes he left them his little gift...

Stan from Wisconsin

Jerry and Bill from Brooklyn, NY

Bud would frequently land on my shoulder and get involved in a phone conversation. One day I was speaking to our tin supplier in Chicago; she also had a bird on her shoulder. Between the two birds chattering, it was hard to get a word in edgewise. Her office parrots sent Bud emails with photos of themselves perched atop her computer.

Bud loved giving manicures and was quite adept at it. He worked on the nails of bankers, lawyers, accountants and diplomats, much to their delight. I called him the meat eater.

Joe, the retired diplomat

Whenever there was a birthday, a card was passed around the office for signing. Bud always signed it in the corner, leaving several little trademark holes from his beak. When school groups came through, he relished being the center of attention, gladly singing to the delight of the children. In addition to the Andy Griffith Show theme song, Bud performed fairly good wolf whistles, the call to arms and a mix of mockingbird tunes. All you had to do to get him to perform was bring out a mirror.

The only times he left my office on his own was if I wasn't there. He might fly down the hallway, turn a sharp corner and land on the shoulder of our customer care specialist, who would then have to explain her cry of surprise to the person she was speaking to on the phone. Fortunately he never tried to fly out my office door that led directly outside, thus he never experienced the perils of true freedom. A saving grace!

Ellen from Maryland

My brother, Paul

Toothpick Legs

One holiday week, I left the office for a meal with my mother who was visiting from North Carolina. Bud flew out into the hallway seeking a friendly shoulder. Due to freshly clipped wings, he couldn't fly as high, so he landed in front of a heavy door which separated our offices from the warehouse. Reggie, one of our shipping clerks, opened the door, resulting in a bird scream, loss of tail feathers and a bloody little leg. I received a call that Bud needed me.

I quickly returned to my office, where Kelley was caretaking poor little Bud in his picnic basket. Kelley was panic-stricken, but I remained unusually calm, knowing I had to get him help fast as blood loss could be fatal. I took him to the local vet who tried several times but was unable to get an accurate x-ray of the tiny little leg. They bandaged his bleeding leg with bright orange tape and referred me to an avian specialist in Virginia Beach. By this time, my husband Jim had shown up to offer support. He drove us the hour across the Chesapeake Bay Bridge-Tunnel.

Jim and Bud watch Animal Planet

As soon as we arrived at the animal hospital, they whisked Bud away. Later we met the vet in an exam room where he placed the x-rays on a light tray. Toothpicks! Bud's little legs looked like toothpicks! "And what is that funny looking lump?" I asked Dr. Fisher, who informed me it was Bud's gizzard. Thankfully, nothing was broken. This close call was almost his final call, but he was going to be OK. We brought him home with a little bandage on his leg and some pain medication.

Bud recovered quickly. He seemed more affectionate than usual, perhaps from all the attention he had received while a patient. After a few days at home in his cottage, he returned to work; everyone was delighted to see him back in my office. Fruits, vegetables and Cheetos® adorned his cage-top playground. Reggie and Kelley were particularly happy to have him back.

One day, during a serious management meeting with our executive team, Bud flew over and landed on a staff member's shoulder. Paul brushed him away and Bud flew back to his cage. This happened again. Bud, not to be outdone, flew back a third time towards Paul's shoulder. Paul held up his file folder, thwarting the attempt. Bud did a quick U-turn and landed back on his perch. Then the

by Buttons

five of us witnessed the closest thing we had ever seen to an avian temper tantrum. Bud fluffed his feathers, shook vigorously, then paced back and forth hissing and screeching loudly -- he was really aggravated. We laughed until we cried, our meeting lost all seriousness.

Realizing how close I had come to losing him, I became even more attentive, taking Bud for a ride on my shoulder when I went to meet with other staff members. He visited our retail shop and entertained our customers more often. Bud and his little toothpick legs...

Reflections

A year after the near-fatal door accident, I ran into Allen from the radio station at the Eastern Shore's annual Harvest Festival and cheerily said, "Hello, Snake Man." This little informal greeting had been going on for well over 12 years.

The next morning, I entered my unusually quiet office; there was no good morning kiss. Bud was sitting on top of his cage, shivering and weak. I immediately knew something was wrong. Old age didn't enter my mind, however. He was over fifteen years old, but he had been so happy and healthy that I just assumed he would be around forever.

My husband took him across the Chesapeake Bay Bridge-Tunnel to the vet we had visited the previous year. I remained at work and tried to concentrate on critical business projects, but it was difficult. I was really worried. They kept Bud overnight for observation and tests. The next morning Dr. Fisher called and told me Bud was experiencing liver failure. They would run some more tests and keep him a second night.

The following day Dr. Fisher called and said Bud's condition had improved and he could come home. When he brought my bird into the waiting room, Bud cheerfully hopped up onto my shoulder and nibbled at my earring, obviously happy to see me. I was so relieved. The vet gave us milk thistle to help his liver. We stopped at a grocery store in Virginia Beach where Jim bought some fresh potatoes and broccoli. We were so hopeful.

Arriving home, I took Bud to his cottage while Jim made mashed potatoes. We wanted Bud to enjoy his favorite foods; however, he didn't have an appetite. That evening I kissed Bud good night and covered his cage with the blue cloth. I didn't sleep well at all. In the morning, when I uncovered his cage, Bud was sitting upright on his perch, leaning against the side. He had passed away peacefully in his sleep. *Oh my Bud*, I cried aloud. He had come home to die.

I was devastated. This little bird had been a part of my life for over fourteen years. Memories rushed forth with my tears: *The first day I got him was the last day I ever saw my father.* Crying, I went to the attic, seeking an appropriate container for burial. I returned with a small elongated cardboard box. Jim decided it wasn't good enough; he went to the attic and came down with a metal Glenfiddich® Scotch box. It was a perfect fit. We placed Bud's favorite mirror along with a photo and a short story about his life in the box, then wrapped him in an antique pink handkerchief.

Reggie and Kelley, both witnesses to Bud's accident the previous year, came over for an impromptu afternoon funeral in our garden. We spoke a few words in memory of Bud then buried him in his Scotch box. Back at work, we placed a photo of Bud in the Eastern Shore News with his obituary. For an entire week we played a DVD of his photos in our shop. We donated a portion of proceeds from shop sales to our local SPCA and also collected contributions in a jar with Bud's photo on it. Word got out, and sympathy emails, cards and contributions poured in from friends, suppliers and customers.

"If love could have saved you, you would have lived forever."

Epilogue

Not long after, I received mail from my friends Ray and Paula with photos of their cockatiel, General, walking around on the floor with their two dogs and two cats. *Now that's real trust*, I say to myself.

Once you love a bird, you quickly learn to overlook little things, like leaving work with bird poop on the rear of your jacket and not being told until you meet someone for dinner at a fancy restaurant. Just one of the joys you overlook, and then miss. Sometimes I would find the dusty print of angel wings on a window that Bud had left behind.

Although several years have passed, children continue to show up at my office door, inquiring, "Where's Bud?" I feel the same way when I arrive to my quiet office. Of all the pets I've had, Bud's loss hurts the most. Every time I hear a mockingbird singing in our yard, I hear Bud. I know he's out there somewhere.

I was sorry to read of the loss of Bud. Only someone who has been loved by a little bundle of feathers can understand the loss of that kind of companionship. I work at a vet hospital where we see many birds. I have a warm spot for cockatiels and have two little rescues of my own. Before meeting my guys, I never realized what joy a little bird could bring! Sounds like Bud had a full, wonderful life. Michele

I am so sorry to hear of the demise of Bud the Bird. I will always remember him whistling happily on the porch with Gardenia fragrance on the breezes! Larry

So sorry Pam. I know what it is like to lose a beloved member of the family and how hard it is to explain sorrow for an animal. I hope you know that the greatest gift in the world for Bud was how much you loved him. And he knew it. I'm sure he was a very happy bird throughout his life with you. Love, Lois

I remember walking into your office and Bud landing on my shoulder pecking my ear. You said to pet him and he loved it. He did that every time I came in. Until then I never cared for birds. Ray

In memory of my bird, Bud
1991 - 2006

Acknowledgments

Many thanks to Caroline Teeling for book design, Ann Hayden, Deb Torguson Pollio and Mary Atkinson for editing, Buttons Boggs for artwork, Wayne Prince for poetry, and everyone who took photos over the years. To the Blue Crab Bay staff and my husband Jim, who took care of Bud and put up with his noise, my gratitude. To Frank and Kelley, thanks for making him your own. And to Boo, thanks for the bird of my life.